Cornw
Beaches

The guide to THE BEST

Jennie Hughes Jones

For further information of all the titles in this series please visit:-
www.tormark.co.uk

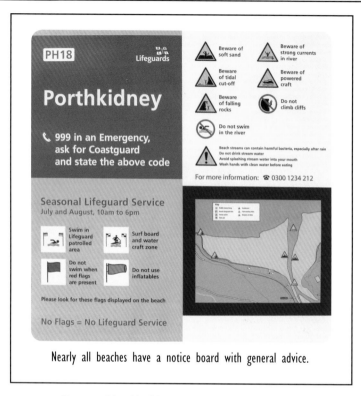

Nearly all beaches have a notice board with general advice.

Designed by Alix Wood, www.alixwood.co.uk

Published by Tor Mark, United Downs Ind Est, Redruth,
Cornwall TR16 5HY

First published 2010
This reprint 2015

© 2010 Jennie Hughes Jones
Photographs © 2010 Alan Hughes Jones
RNLI Photograph (page 48) © Andrew Stanton
Cover Photograph © Shutterstock 2015

ISBN 978 085025 422 8

Printed by Booths Print, The Praze, Penryn, Cornwall TR10 8AA

FOREWORD

While compiling this guide I have tried to incorporate all the elements needed for a good day at the beach for everyone. Be you a surfer, a family or a wildlife enthusiast, you will find beaches and coves that suit you. I have also included disabled beach lovers and dog owners in the hunt for a good beach. In this high tech world, it seemed only right to include information for Sat Nav plus OS map grid references and the usual written directions to the beaches. The post codes for Sat Nav will take you to nearest building to the beach or car park, by then you should be able to see the beach or signs for it.

Most important of all I have included everything you need to keep yourself and your family safe, remembering that the seaside is a potentially dangerous place if not respected. Cornwall lovers will see that I have not included all of the 200+ beaches and coves. I decided to concentrate on the more accessible ones, the rest require long walks or steep descents, and are not easily accessed by surfers or families carrying the paraphernalia required for a day at the beach. I decided to leave them to the coastal path walkers.

Following the awful storms of winter 2014 the sand levels have changed on many Cornish beaches, in some cases drastically. This has caused rip currents to appear in places not previously experienced.

If you are on holiday and intend to surf ask the lifeguards or a local surfer for advice. In the autum of 2014 as this new edition was being prepared two locals lost their lives in trying to save four teenage surfers who fortunately survived. The sea is a dangerous place — please take care.

BLUE FLAG BEACHES

Blue Flag is an international scheme which acts as a guarantee to tourists that a beach they are visiting is one of the best in the world.
It is awarded to coastal destinations which have achieved the highest quality in water facilities, safety, environmental education and management.
These beaches are being constantly re-assessed and their status can change.
Therefore we have not included details of Blue Flag Beaches in Cornwall.
If you would like further information please go to:-
www.blueflag.org.uk

WATER QUALITY   www.defra.gov.uk

① SANDYMOUTH BAY

This large sandy beach with plenty of sand at low tide has many interesting rock formations and rock pools. Strong currents.

Comments:
Check Tide Table. Unstable cliffs. Risk of being cut off. Be wary at low tide.

P Parking   One NT car park
T Toilets   Yes — No Disabled
F Facilities Shop, Café
A Activities Surfing
S Safety   Lifeguards in summer
D Dogs   Allowed all year
D Disabled   No beach access

Directions: A39 from Wadebridge or Camelford just before Kilkhampton turn left and shortly after Stibb, turn left for Sandy Mouth. Beach just past the Sandymouth Holiday Park.

Post Code: EX23 9HW
OS Grid Ref: SS203100

② NORTHCOTT MOUTH

A large sandy beach which extends into a much bigger beach with rock pools at low tide.

Comments:
Swimming and surfing considered unsafe.

P Parking   NT car park 40 spaces
T Toilets   No. Toilets at Poughill + Disabled
F Facilities Margaret's Tea Garden near beach
A Activities Surfing — experienced only
S Safety   Lifeguards in summer
D Dogs   Allowed all year
D Disabled   Beach access on steep path

Directions: Take A39 from Wadebridge or Camelford. Just after Bude and Stratton turn left at crossroad signed Poughill. At Poughill turn right, ½ ml later then right again, follow road to Northcott Mouth.

Post Code: EX23 9ED
OS Grid Ref: SS202085

③ CROOKLETS BEACH, BUDE

A large sandy beach popular with families and less experienced surfers. Some visiting Aussies christened it "The Bondi of Britain".

Comments:
Swimming unsafe at low tide.
Home of Bude Life Saving Club.

Directions: Take A39 to Bude, follow signs for beaches in centre.

P Parking	One car park 320 spaces
T Toilets	Yes + Disabled
F Facilities	Shop, Cafés, Amusements
A Activities	Surfing, Play area
S Safety	Lifeguards in summer
D Dogs	Banned Easter to Oct 1st
D Disabled	Beach access

Post Code: EX23 8NE
OS Grid Ref: SS203072

---

④ SUMMERLEAZE BEACH, BUDE

This beach, one of the two main beaches in Bude, is a sand and shingle beach backed by sand dunes and cliffs.

Comments:
Swimming can be unsafe at low tide.

Directions: Take A39 to Bude turn off, follow signs for Bude and beaches in centre.

P Parking	Large car park by beach, another one by canal bridge
T Toilets	Yes + Disabled
F Facilities	Shops, Café etc
A Activities	Surfing, Canoeing
S Safety	Lifeguards in summer
D Dogs	Allowed all year on leads
D Disabled	Disabled beach access. Sand chair hire

Post Code: EX23 8JY
OS Grid Ref: SS208065

5 WIDEMOUTH BAY

This mile long sandy beach is backed by low cliffs and has many rock pools to explore and is very popular with families and surfers.

Comments:
Swimming unsafe due to strong currents.

P Parking   Various car parks 1000 spaces
T Toilets   Yes + Disabled
F Facilities   Shop, Café, Surf Hire
A Activities   Surfing
S Safety   Lifeguards in summer
D Dogs   Banned Easter to Oct 1st - North beach only. South beach allowed all year
D Disabled   Beach access

Directions: From Bude on the A39 and follow signs for Widemouth Bay.

Post Code: EX23 0AW
OS Grid Ref: SS199028

6 CRACKINGTON HAVEN

A small sandy beach surrounded by 400 ft cliffs and with plenty of rock pools to explore.

Comments:
Swimmers keep to centre of beach. Avoid southern side at all times.

P Parking   Two car parks 50 spaces
T Toilets   Yes + Disabled
F Facilities   Cafés, Pub, Ice-cream kiosk
A Activities   Surfing
S Safety   Lifeguards in summer
D Dogs   Banned Easter to Oct 1st
D Disabled   No beach access

Directions: Nearest town Tintagel. A39 north turn left at Wainhouse Corner and follow this road.

Post Code: EX23 0JG
OS Grid Ref: SX143968

⑦ TREBARWITH STRAND

This large stretch of sandy beach is popular with surfers and families alike, although completely covered at high tide. Access unsuitable for wheelchairs.

Comments:
Swimming 2 hours either side of low tide unsafe. Consult Tide Table.

Directions: Nearest town is Tintagel. B3263 just before entering Tintagel, follow signs to the beach.

P Parking	One car park 50 spaces 5min walk
T Toilets	Yes + Disabled
F Facilities	Shops, Cafés, Surf hire and school
A Activities	Surfing
S Safety	Lifeguards in summer
D Dogs	Allowed all year
D Disabled	No beach access

Post Code: PL 34 0HB
OS Grid Ref: SX050863

info.co.uk/trebarwithstrand

---

⑧ POLZEATH

A hugely popular family beach, with rock pools at low tide. Considered to be one of the best surfing beaches in Cornwall, but very crowded in season. Access via slipway.

Comments:
Young children should be watched at all times due to the volume of surfers in the water.

Directions: Nearest town is Wadebridge. Take B3314 to Polzeath. Route is signed.

P Parking	On beach or top of hill
T Toilets	Yes + Disabled
F Facilities	Shops, Cafes, Bars, Restaurants
A Activities	Surfing, Surf hire, Canoeing, Sailing
S Safety	Lifeguards in summer
D Dogs	Banned Easter to Oct 1st
D Disabled	Beach access. Sand Chair hire

Post Code: PL27 6TD
OS Grid Ref: SW934789

www.polzeath.co.uk

9 DAYMER BAY

A sandy beach with rock pools, although at mouth of Camel Estuary, still very pleasant. It is backed by sand dunes and access is via steps.

Comments:
Surfboards and speedboats banned, swimming unsafe at low tide due to strong currents.

P Parking   One large car park by beach
T Toilets   Yes + Disabled
F Facilities Shop, Café
A Activities Windsurfing
S Safety   No Lifeguards
D Dogs   Allowed all year
D Disabled   No beach access

Directions: Wadebridge to Polzeath road. Turn left to Rock and right into Trewiston.

Post Code: PL27 6SA
OS Grid Ref: SW929776

10 ROCK

There is a long sandy beach on each side of Rock on the Camel Estuary, with extensive sand dunes.

Comments:
Unsafe for snorkelling and surfing due to strong currents and river traffic.

P Parking   One and some road parking
T Toilets   Yes + Disabled at Daymer Bay
F Facilities Shops, Cafes, Bars, Restaurants
A Activities Boating, Fishing trips
S Safety   No Lifeguards
D Dogs   Allowed on leads
D Disabled   Beach access

Directions: From Wadebridge take B3314 to St Minver. Just before St Minver turn left for Rock.

Post Code: PL27 6LD
OS Grid Ref: SW928757

www.rockincornwall.co.uk

11 TREVONE BAY

This popular sandy family beach is surrounded by cliffs. Access via gentle slope and steps from car park. Close by a rocky beach with a tidal pool.

Comments:
Strong currents make swimming unsafe, keep to centre of beach.

P Parking   Two car parks 500 spaces
T Toilets   Yes + Disabled
F Facilities   Café, Restaurant, Surf hire
A Activities   Surfing
S Safety   Lifeguards in summer
D Dogs   Banned Easter to Oct 1st
D Disabled   Beach access possible

Directions: A389 for Padstow, just before Padstow turn left onto B3276, follow this road until turning for Trevone Bay.

Post Code: PL28 8QX
OS Grid Ref: SW892758

12 HARLYN BAY

This could be said to be one of the best beaches in Cornwall. A spacious sandy beach, popular with families and surfers. Access at various places along the dunes.

Comments:
A quiet sheltered spot with good cliff walks.

P Parking   Yes, with field parking in season
T Toilets   Yes + Disabled
F Facilities   Shop, Café, Pub, Surf hire
A Activities   Surfing, Sailing & Canoeing
S Safety   Lifeguards in summer
D Dogs   Allowed all year
D Disabled   Beach access

Directions: Directions: A389 for Padstow, just before Padstow turn left onto B3276 Stay on this road until a right turn for Harlyn Bay.

Post Code: PL28 8SB
OS Grid Ref: SW876752

13 CONSTANTINE BAY

A wide sandy bay with many rock pools and large sand dunes to explore. Access is via a sloping path down to the beach.

Comments:
Swimming unsafe due to strong currents, signs show safe areas.

P Parking   26 + 300 extra in season
T Toilets   Yes + Disabled
F Facilities   Surf hire, Shop in village
A Activities   Surfing
S Safety   Lifeguards in summer, Lost Child Centre
D Dogs   Allowed all year
D Disabled   Beach access

Directions: From Padstow take B3276, just after St Merryn turn right for Constantine Bay, past Treyglos Hotel.

Post Code: PL28 8JH
OS Grid Ref: SW865743

---

14 TREYARNON BAY

A small sandy cove with rocky outcrops and rock pools. A natural tidal pool at low tide makes swimming safe for small children. Access by slipway.

Comments:
Swimmers: keep to centre of beach, large breaking waves and strong currents.

P Parking   One car park, 480 spaces
T Toilets   Yes + Disabled
F Facilities   Shop, Café, Restaurants, Surf hire
A Activities   Surfing
S Safety   Lifeguards in summer, Lost Child Centre
D Dogs   Allowed all year
D Disabled   Beach access

Directions: From Padstow take B3276, just after St Merryn turn right for Treyarnon Bay.

Post Code: PL28 8JR
OS Grid Ref: SW858745

15 PORTHCOTHAN BAY

A popular family beach with grassy sand dunes and plenty of sand at low tide. Access to beach is level.

Comments:
Swimming safer in centre of beach. Currents make it dangerous.

P	Parking	One car park
T	Toilets	Yes + Disabled
F	Facilities	Café, Restaurant
A	Activities	Surfing
S	Safety	Lifeguards in summer
D	Dogs	Allowed all year
D	Disabled	Beach access

Directions: From Padstow take B3276, past Watergate Bay through Mawgan Porth. Approx 3 miles later arrive at Porthcothan.

Post Code: PL28 8LW
OS Grid Ref: SW858719

www.porthcothan.co.uk

---

16 MAWGAN PORTH

A large sandy beach with sand dunes and a even larger expanse of sand at low tide. Access to beach is level.

Comments: Nearest town Newquay (5 miles).

P	Parking	Two car parks 240 spaces
T	Toilets	Yes + Disabled
F	Facilities	Café, Pub, Beach shops
A	Activities	Surfing, Sailing
S	Safety	Lifeguards in summer
D	Dogs	Allowed all year
D	Disabled	Beach access

Directions: Follow B3276 past Watergate Bay and on to Mawgan Porth.

Post Code: TR8 4BA
OS Grid Ref: SW849671

17 WATERGATE BAY

This excellent sandy beach is good for surfing and families. It can be accessed from various points, but most facilities are by the Watergate Hotel.

Comments:
Fast incoming tides here. Good for surfing beginners.

P Parking   Two car parks – 120 spaces
T Toilets   Yes + Disabled at Tolcarne Beach (see No 20 opposite)
F Facilities   Shop, Café, Jamie Oliver's 15
A Activities   Surfing, Surf school
S Safety   Lifeguards in summer
D Dogs   Allowed all year
D Disabled   Beach access

Directions: take B3276 from Padstow to Newquay and follow signs to Watergate Bay.

Post Code: TR8 4AA
OS Grid Ref: SW841649

18 PORTH BEACH – NEWQUAY

This reasonably flat sandy beach is popular with families with young children, as the shallow water makes paddling and swimming easier.

Comments:
Avoid swimming on north side of beach.

P Parking   Yes opposite beach + road
T Toilets   Yes + Disabled at Tolcarne
F Facilities   Shop, Café, Pub
A Activities   Pitch & Putt, Crazy Golf, Swimming
S Safety   Lifeguards in summer
D Dogs   Banned Easter to Oct 1st
D Disabled   Beach access easy

Directions: Beach is ¾ mile from Newquay, with direct access from road.

Post Code: TR7 3NE
OS Grid Ref: SW830626

19 LUSTY GLAZE – NEWQUAY

This is a beautiful sandy beach in a private cove, overlooked by steep cliffs. On the outskirts of Newquay, a popular family beach.

Comments:
You can walk along beach from Newquay.

P Parking   Yes top of cliff
T Toilets   Yes + Disabled in Newquay
F Facilities   Café, Surf hire
A Activities   Surfing, Fishing Canoeing
S Safety   No Lifeguards
D Dogs   Banned Easter to Oct 1st
D Disabled   No beach access

Directions: Just off B3058 follow signs from Newquay on north eastern side.

Post Code: TR7 1HD
OS Grid Ref: SW808618

www.lustyglaze.co.uk

20 TOLCARNE BEACH – NEWQUAY

A large expanse of sand makes this a popular beach. It is surrounded by a horseshoe of steep cliffs.

Comments:
Drop off point by beach for disabled.

P Parking   Yes 5 min walk from town parking
T Toilets   Yes + Disabled by entrance
F Facilities   Café, Shop, Surf hire, Beach huts
A Activities   Surfing, Swimming
S Safety   Lifeguards in summer
D Dogs   Banned Easter to Oct 1st
D Disabled   Beach access easy

Directions: Access from Newquay beach road by steps or access road.

Post Code: TR7 2QN
OS Grid Ref: SW817620

㉑ GREAT WESTERN BEACH – NEWQUAY

Right in the centre of Newquay, this is the quietest beach, backed by sheer cliffs, it is a sandy beach with outcrops of rocks.

Comments:
Car drop off point at beach for disabled. Good waves for experienced surfers.

Directions: A town beach. Access is by steps or the access road.

P Parking Car park spaces in Newquay
T Toilets Yes + Disabled
F Facilities Café, Restaurant, Sunbeds
A Activities Surfing. Swimming, Sailing
S Safety Lifeguards in summer
D Dogs Allowed all year
D Disabled Beach access by steep path

Post Code: TR7 2NE
OS Grid Ref: SW815618

㉒ TOWAN BEACH – NEWQUAY

This is considered the family beach of Newquay, situated by the harbour; it is mostly used by surfing beginners and swimmers.

Comments:
Sand Chair Hire 01637 878134.

Directions: Between Gt. Western and Fistral on the beach road.

P Parking Yes in Newquay
T Toilets Yes + Disabled in Newquay
F Facilities Café, Surf hire
A Activities Surfing, Swimming
S Safety Lifeguards in summer
D Dogs Allowed all year
D Disabled Beach access

Post Code: TR7 1HD
OS Grid Ref: SW808618

FISTRAL BEACH – NEWQUAY

A large sandy beach with rock pools and sand dunes. A popular surfing beach, it is often the venue for the World Surfing Championships.

Comments:
Long boards can unintentionally be a hazard to swimmers and unsupervised young children. Rip currents make swimming dangerous for young children.

Directions: Fistral is ½ mile from Newquay on the seafront.

P	Parking	Car parking in Newquay centre
T	Toilets	Yes + Disabled in Newquay
F	Facilities	Café, Restaurant, Surf hire
A	Activities	Surfing
S	Safety	Lifeguards in summer
D	Dogs	Allowed all year
D	Disabled	Beach access. Sand Chair Hire

Post Code: TR7 1HY
OS Grid Ref: SW801622

www.fistralbeach.com

 # CRANTOCK BEACH – NEWQUAY

A huge sandy beach with steep cliffs at one end and sand dunes at the other. River runs down side of beach, bathing not allowed in it.

Comments:
Swimming can be unsafe due to strong currents and rip currents.

Directions: Access is via Crantock Village, just south of Newquay. Follow signs to beach.

P	Parking	NT car park behind dunes
T	Toilets	Yes + Disabled in Newquay
F	Facilities	Café, Surf hire, Ice cream van
A	Activities	Surfing, Canoeing, Swimming
S	Safety	Lifeguards in summer
		Read safety rules displayed
D	Dogs	Allowed all year
D	Disabled	Beach access difficult

Post Code: TR8 5RN
OS Grid Ref: SW789609

25 PORTH JOKE BEACH

Narrow sandy cove with caves and rock pools. Porth Joke is sometimes known as Polly Joke by the locals.

Comments:
Private beach accessed via farm. Please close gates.

P Parking   NT car park
T Toilets   Campsite by farm
F Facilities   Treago Farm Shop
A Activities   Surfing, Swimming
S Safety   No Lifeguards. Good beach, but isolated
D Dogs   Dogs allowed all year
D Disabled   No beach access

Directions: From the A30 take the B3285. Then take B3075 for Goonhaven approx. 3 miles later turn left for Treago Farm, drive through the farm. Beach is accessed via a gate in the car park. Follow the narrow path to the beach.

Post Code: TR8 5QS
OS Grid Ref: SW781600

26 HOLYWELL BAY

This large sandy beach is very popular with families and surfers alike. The beach has a large amount of sand dunes, rock pools and caves to explore.

Comments:
Beware of getting cut off by incoming tide when exploring the caves. Check Tide Tables.

P Parking   NT car park 5 min walk
T Toilets   Yes but no Disabled Toilets
F Facilities   Beach Shop
A Activities   Cliff Walking, Swimming, Surfing, Rock pools, Caving
S Safety   Lifeguards in summer
D Dogs   Anytime
D Disabled   No beach access

Directions: A30, turn North onto the B3285 to Goonhaven, then turn right onto the B3075. After 2 miles turn left onto road signposted Cubert and Holywell Bay.

Post Code: TR8 5PP
OS Grid Ref: SW768588

27 PERRANPORTH

A very popular family beach backed by sand dunes. The sand is flat, making the sea very shallow and safer for younger children. Far end of beach is an unofficial nudist area.

Comments:
Be aware that the tide comes in very fast here.

P Parking   Three car parks
T Toilets   By beach + Disabled
F Facilities   Shops, Restaurants, Pubs, Cafés
A Activities   Surfing
S Safety   Lifeguards in summer
D Dogs   Dogs allowed all year - on lead in designated areas
D Disabled   Beach access

Directions: B3277 straight into village and follow the signs for beach and car parks.

Post Code: TR6 0DN
OS Grid Ref: SW759543

28 TREVAUNANCE COVE

A beautiful sandy cove surrounded by tall cliffs with plenty of rock pools to explore. Slipway.

Comments:
Beware of unstable cliffs. Do not sit under them or climb them.

P Parking   Two car parks
T Toilets   Yes + Disabled
F Facilities   Café, Pub, Restaurants, RNLI shop
A Activities   Surfing, Canoeing
S Safety   Lifeguards in summer
D Dogs   Dogs allowed all year on leads
D Disabled   Beach access

Directions: A30 to Chiverton roundabout. Take B3277 to St Agnes Go through village (one way system) and take first left after the Peterville Inn to the cove.

Post Code: TR5 0RU
OS Grid Ref: SW722515

29 CHAPEL PORTH

A small rock and shingle cove extending to a huge sandy beach as tide recedes, rock pools and caves to explore.

Comments:
Risk of being cut off. Consult Tide Table.

P Parking	NT car park 80 spaces. In season parking top of hill – steep climb back
T Toilets	Yes, but no disabled
F Facilities	Café, their hedgehog ice creams are legendary
A Activities	Surfing
S Safety	Lifeguards in summer
D Dogs	Banned Easter to Oct 1st
D Disabled	Beach access very difficult

Directions: A30 to Chiverton Roundabout, take B3277 to St Agnes, turn left at mini roundabout and follow the road to Chapel Porth.

Post Code: TR5 0NS
OS Grid Ref: SW697494

30 PORTHTOWAN

This is a spacious sandy beach popular with families and surfers having level access to the beach.

Comments:
Recommend early arrival as car parks fill quickly.

P Parking	Two car parks, some road parking
T Toilets	Yes + Disabled in car park
F Facilities	Shop, Café, Pub, Surf hire
A Activities	Surfing, Fishing
S Safety	Lifeguards in summer
D Dogs	Banned Easter to Oct 1st
D Disabled	Beach access

Directions: A30 to Chiverton Roundabout, take B3277 for St Agnes, turn left at Sevenmilestone Garage and follow signs.

Post Code: TR4 8AW
OS Grid Ref: SW692481

31 PORTREATH

A small port with a wide sandy beach to the west of the harbour. Left hand side of the beach has caves at low tide.

Comments:
Very popular with surfers at all levels.

P Parking One car park, some road parking
T Toilets Yes + Disabled
F Facilities Café, Shop, Pub
A Activities Surfing, Canoeing, Crazy Golf
S Safety Lifeguards in summer
D Dogs Banned Easter to Oct 1st
D Disabled Beach access

Directions: A30 to Redruth exit, take right hand lane (double roundabout) Follow round to Portreath exit, then follow signs.

Post Code: TR16 4NN
OS Grid Ref: SW653453

32 GODREVY BEACH

This is a huge sandy beach with stunning views. It is made up of stretches of sandy beach with rock pools and large rocky outcrops. Access down wooden steps.

Comments:
Signs warn of strong currents and risk of being cut off.

P Parking NT car park on cliff top
T Toilets Yes + Disabled in car park - both seasonal
F Facilities Café in first car park
A Activities Surfing
S Safety Lifeguards in summer
D Dogs Banned Easter to Oct 1st
D Disabled No beach access

Directions: A30 to Loggans Moor Roundabout. Take Hayle exit, then turn right at mini roundabout after Lidl. Follow road to bridge over Red River, turn left for car parks.

Post Code: TR27 5ED
OS Grid Ref: SW584421

Owing to recent landslips this beach could be closed at any time. Please ring 01208 265200 for advice.

33 GWITHIAN TOWANS

A huge sandy beach, popular with families and surfers, next to Hayle Sands.

Comments:
There are sand dunes ending in 30ft cliffs, which are crumbling and dangerous.

P Parking   One large, two small
T Toilets   Yes + Disabled at Godrevy
F Facilities   Licensed Café, Surf shop
A Activities   Surfing
S Safety   Lifeguards in summer
D Dogs   Banned Easter to Oct 1st
D Disabled   No beach access

Directions: A30 to Loggans Moor Roundabout take exit for Hayle, past Lidl and turn right at mini roundabout onto B3301. Follow this road and turn left after Atlantic Sands Caravan Park.

Post Code: TR27 5BW
OS Grid Ref: SW585406

www.gwithian.org.uk

34 HAYLE SANDS

This is a huge stretch of sand which consists of Hayle Towans, Black Cliff and Mexico Towans, all popular surfing beaches.

Comments:
Popular beaches with experienced surfers.

P Parking   Across road from pub
T Toilets   Yes, but no Disabled
F Facilities   Pub, Café, Surf Life Saving Club
A Activities   Surfing
S Safety   Lifeguards in summer
D Dogs   Banned Easter to Oct 1st. Allowed all year on Mexico Beach
D Disabled   Beach access difficult

Directions: A30 to Loggans Moor Roundabout Take exit for Hayle, straight over mini roundabout, take second right turn to Phillack. Road ends in pub car park Public car park on other side of the road.

Post Code: TR27 5AP
OS Grid Ref: SW563392

35 CARBIS BAY

This lovely beach of golden sand is privately owned by the Carbis Bay Hotel. Sheltered by high cliffs it is a great favourite with young families. Access via a slipway.

Comments:
Access to hotel bar from beach.

P Parking	Car park by beach - expensive
T Toilets	Yes + Disabled at hotel - permission given
F Facilities	Shop, Café, Takeaway
A Activities	Swimming, Surfing
S Safety	Lifeguards in summer
D Dogs	Banned Easter to Oct 1st
D Disabled	Beach access

Directions: From A30, take B3074 through Lelant. As you enter Carbis Bay there is a right turn just before the pedestrian lights signed to the beach.

Post Code: TR26 2NP
OS Grid Ref: SW526389

36 PORTHMINSTER – ST IVES

A large perfect sandy beach on the southern edge of St Ives, backed by palm trees and tropical plants, on a hot day you could be in the Med.

Comments:
Sand Chair Hire 01736 793940.

P Parking	Yes, near Railway Station
T Toilets	Yes + Disabled in car park
F Facilities	Café, Restaurant, Beach huts etc
A Activities	Swimming
S Safety	Lifeguards in summer
D Dogs	Banned 24/7
	Dog friendly Porthkidney Lelant - 3 miles
D Disabled	Beach access

Directions: A30, then B3074 to St Ives follow signs for Railway Station car park. Beach is below car park – fills up very early – use Park & Ride. (See No. 37 overleaf)

Post Code: TR26 2EQ
OS Grid Ref: SW520400

37 HARBOUR BEACH – ST IVES

This beach is located in the harbour and is popular with families. The beach is very flat and so the sea is shallow for quite a distance.

Comments:

Parking in St Ives is very limited. Park & Ride drops you 2 mins from harbour.

P Parking	Park & Ride
T Toilets	Yes + Disabled behind Sloop Inn
F Facilities	Shops, Cafés, Restaurants, Pubs
A Activities	Boat trips, Fishing trips
S Safety	No Lifeguards
D Dogs	Banned Easter to Oct 1st
	Dog friendly Lambeth Beach - behind RNLI
D Disabled	Beach access

Directions: A30 to B3074. At mini roundabout bear left on B3311 at 2nd mini roundabout take sharp left, follow this road to t-junction, turn right and follow signs for Park & Ride.

Post Code: TR26 1HB
OS Grid Ref: SW514401

38 PORTHGWIDDEN BEACH – ST IVES

A small beach to the north of St Ives Harbour, very popular with families with young children. Car park above the beach, but invariably full – use Park & Ride.

Comments:

Just around the corner the tiny beach of Bamaluz.

P Parking	Park & Ride
T Toilets	Yes + Disabled at Porthmeor
F Facilities	Café/Bar, Shop, Beach huts
A Activities	Swimming
S Safety	No Lifeguards
D Dogs	Banned 24/7
	Dog friendly Bamaluz beach next door
D Disabled	Steep beach access

Directions: A30 to B3074, at mini roundabout-bear left on B3311, at 2nd roundabout take sharp left, follow this road to a T-Junction, turn right and follow signs for Park & Ride.

Post Code: TR26 1HB
OS Grid Ref: SW514401

39 PORTHMEOR BEACH – ST IVES

The best surfing beach in St Ives, this wide sandy beach is very popular with families and surfers. Access via steps or slipway.

Comments:
St Ives has very little central parking. Park & Ride drops you in the centre.

P Parking Park & Ride
T Toilets Yes + Disabled
F Facilities Café/Bar, Tate Gallery
A Activities Surfing, Windsurfing, Canoeing
S Safety Lifeguards in summer
D Dogs Banned 24/7
D Disabled Beach access

Directions: A30 to B3074. At mini roundabout bear left on B3311 at 2nd mini roundabout take sharp left, follow this road to t-junction, turn right and follow signs for Park & Ride.

Post Code: TR26 1HB
OS Grid Ref: SW514401

40 SENNEN COVE

A wide sandy beach, popular with families and all levels of surfers. Far end of beach is an unofficial nudist beach.

Comments:
Just one mile east of Land's End and its attractions.

P Parking Two car parks by the beach; field at the top of the steep hill in season
T Toilets Yes + Disabled
F Facilities Cafés, Restaurants
A Activities Surfing, Sailing, Canoeing
S Safety Lifeguards in summer
D Dogs Banned Easter to Oct 1st
D Disabled Beach access

Directions: Take A30 round outskirts of Penzance heading for Lands End, just before Lands End turn right for Sennen Cove.

Post Code: TR19 7DJ
OS Grid Ref: SW354263

www.sennencove.com

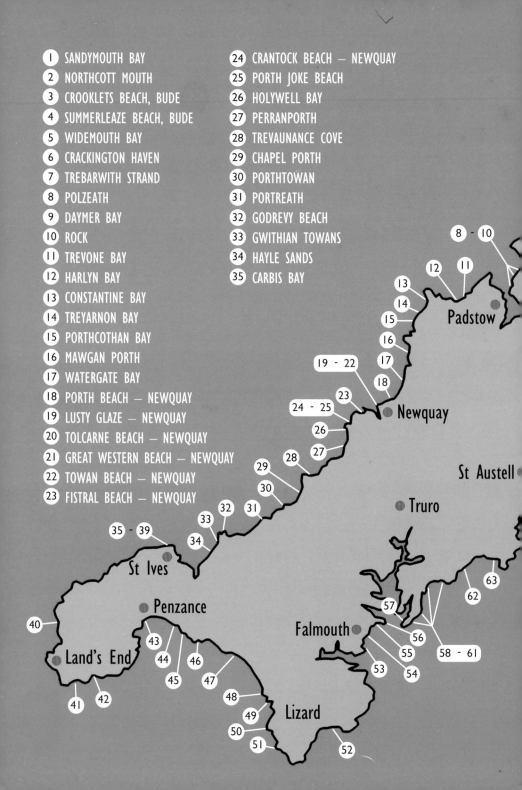

1 SANDYMOUTH BAY
2 NORTHCOTT MOUTH
3 CROOKLETS BEACH, BUDE
4 SUMMERLEAZE BEACH, BUDE
5 WIDEMOUTH BAY
6 CRACKINGTON HAVEN
7 TREBARWITH STRAND
8 POLZEATH
9 DAYMER BAY
10 ROCK
11 TREVONE BAY
12 HARLYN BAY
13 CONSTANTINE BAY
14 TREYARNON BAY
15 PORTHCOTHAN BAY
16 MAWGAN PORTH
17 WATERGATE BAY
18 PORTH BEACH — NEWQUAY
19 LUSTY GLAZE — NEWQUAY
20 TOLCARNE BEACH — NEWQUAY
21 GREAT WESTERN BEACH — NEWQUAY
22 TOWAN BEACH — NEWQUAY
23 FISTRAL BEACH — NEWQUAY

24 CRANTOCK BEACH — NEWQUAY
25 PORTH JOKE BEACH
26 HOLYWELL BAY
27 PERRANPORTH
28 TREVAUNANCE COVE
29 CHAPEL PORTH
30 PORTHTOWAN
31 PORTREATH
32 GODREVY BEACH
33 GWITHIAN TOWANS
34 HAYLE SANDS
35 CARBIS BAY

Padstow

8 - 10
12
11
13
14
15
16
17
18
19 - 22
23
24 - 25
26
27
28
29
30
31
32
33
34
35 - 39

Newquay

St Austell

Truro

St Ives

Penzance

Falmouth

57
62
63
56
55
58 - 61
53
54

Land's End

40
43
44
45
46
47
48
49
50
51
41
42
52

Lizard

● Bude

● Tintagel

● Launceston

● Wadebridge

● Bodmin

Saltash ●

41 PORTHGWARRA

A small fishing village, now sadly reduced to one boat. This lovely cove has a steep slipway and sandy beach. Nearby steep cliffs are used by expert climbers and for Commando Training.

Comments:
Lobster and mackerel fishing

P Parking	One small car park
T Toilets	Yes
F Facilities	Shop/Café
A Activities	Fishing, Swimming
S Safety	No lifeguards
D Dogs	Banned Easter to Oct 1st
D Disabled	Beach access difficult

Directions: Take A30 towards Land's End, 2 miles after Penzance turn left onto B3283 through St Buryan when B3283 joins B3315 take B3315 through Treen, turn left for Porthgwarra.

Post Code: TR19 6JR
OS Grid Ref: SW372218

42 PORTHCURNO

One of Cornwall's most beautiful beaches surrounded by granite cliffs and smaller coves at low tide. With its golden sand and jade green sea it is very popular with families.

Comments:
There are strong currents and rip currents. World famous Minack Theatre on cliffs above beach.

P Parking	One large car park
T Toilets	Yes + Disabled in car park
F Facilities	Shops, Cafés, Pub
A Activities	Surfing, Swimming, Snorkelling
S Safety	Lifeguards in summer
D Dogs	Banned Easter to Oct 1st
D Disabled	Beach access

Directions: Take the A30 towards Lands End 2 miles after Penzance take B3283 through St Buryan, then take B3315 through Treen, turn left to Porthcurno.

Post Code: TR17 0AB
OS Grid Ref: SW514311

43 PENZANCE PROMENADE

Penzance is a busy seaside town with all the usual facilities. The beach is sand and shingle and there is access at various places.

Comments:
There is an open air swimming pool along the seafront.

P Parking   Car Parks on seafront
T Toilets   Yes + Disabled at Railway Station
F Facilities   Shops, Cafés Etc.
A Activities   Swimming
S Safety   No Lifeguards
D Dogs   Banned Easter to Oct 1st
D Disabled   No beach access

Directions: Take the A30 into Penzance and follow signs for the seafront and to the promenade.

Post Code: TR18 4DL
OS Grid Ref: SW472298

44 MARAZION

A long sand and pebble beach, stretches at low tide to Penzance. A gently sloping beach ideal for families. Accessed at various points between Marazion and Penzance.

Comments:
Sand Chair Hire 01736 710202. St Michael's Mount can be reached from here.

P Parking   Car Parks along whole beach
T Toilets   Yes + Disabled at Follyfield Station
F Facilities   Shop, Cafés, Surf hire
A Activities   Windsurfing, Canoeing, Sailing
S Safety   Lifeguards in summer
D Dogs   Banned Easter to Oct 1st
D Disabled   Beach access

Directions: Take A30 towards Penzance. At first roundabout take exit for Marazion, follow this road to the village and car parks.

Post Code: TR17 0EN
OS Grid Ref: SW517305

45 PERRANUTHNOE BEACH

A wide sandy beach close to the village of Perranuthnoe. It is completely covered at high tide. Access via slipway and steps.

Comments:
Surfers be aware that spring tides bring strong currents here.

P Parking   One small car park
T Toilets   Yes, but no Disabled
F Facilities   Café
A Activities   Swimming, Surfing
S Safety   No Lifeguards
D Dogs   Banned Easter to Oct 1st
D Disabled   Beach access

Directions: Take A30 to Penzance, just after Crowlas take 1st exit on roundabout onto A394, approx 2 miles later turn right for Perranuthnoe.

Post Code: TR20 9NE
OS Grid Ref: SW539294

46 PRAA SANDS

A great sandy beach surrounded by cliffs, very popular with families and surfers. Gently sloping beach. Access via a slipway.

Comments:
Great beach for children.

P Parking   Three large car parks
T Toilets   Yes + Disabled
F Facilities   Shop, Café, Restaurant, Surf hire
A Activities   Surfing, Swimming
S Safety   Lifeguards in summer
D Dogs   Banned Easter to Oct 1st
D Disabled   Beach access - very steep slipway

Directions: Take A30 turn onto A394 at Marazion, after Marazion follow signs for Praa Sands.

Post Code: TR20 9TQ
OS Grid Ref: SW578281

47 PORTHLEVEN

A long sand, shingle and rock steeply shelving beach extending for approx 3 miles. Very experienced surfers consider this a great surfing beach. Steep slipway.

Comments:
Unsafe for inexperienced swimmers, shelves steeply; can be very dangerous. Not recommended for children and families.

P	Parking	Small Car Park in village + road
T	Toilets	Yes + Disabled in Shute Lane
F	Facilities	Café, Shops, Pubs
A	Activities	Surfing, Fishing
S	Safety	Lifeguards in summer
D	Dogs	Banned Easter to Oct 1st
D	Disabled	Beach access difficult, but possible

Directions: Take the A394 to the B3304 and follow signs to Porthleven.

Post Code: TR13 9JB
OS Grid Ref: SW628257

---

48 CHURCH COVE – GUNWALLOE

A sand and pebble beach, with rocky outcrops. There is a small church in the corner of the cove.

Comments:
Nearby Dollar Cove. Try your luck finding coins from sunken galleon.

P	Parking	One NT car park
T	Toilets	Yes + Disabled by car park
F	Facilities	Café/Shop - seasonal
A	Activities	Swimming, Surfing
S	Safety	Lifeguards in summer
D	Dogs	Banned Easter to Oct 1st
D	Disabled	Beach access difficult, but possible

Directions: Take A394 to Helston, then follow the A3083 to Lizard, approx 2 miles after Helston turn right for Gunwalloe, follow road to beach.

Post Code: TR12 7QE
OS Grid Ref: SW659207

49 POLDHU COVE

A large sandy beach with sand dunes, making this a popular local beach, level access to the beach.

Comments:
Take care at low tide.

P Parking   One small car park + road
T Toilets   Yes + Disabled by beach
F Facilities   Shop
A Activities   Surfing, Swimming
S Safety   Lifeguards in summer
D Dogs   Banned Easter to Oct 1st
D Disabled   Beach access easy

Directions: Take A394 to Helston, then follow the A3083 to Lizard, approx 2 miles   after Lizard turn right for Cury and Poldhu Cove.

Post Code: TR12 7JF
OS Grid Ref: SW666201

50 MULLION COVE

A picturesque little cove that has a small sandy beach at low tide, within the harbour. Slipway.

Comments:
No parking at harbour.

P Parking   Two Car Parks – 5 mins walk
T Toilets   Yes + Disabled
F Facilities   Café
A Activities   Fishing
S Safety   No Lifeguards
D Dogs   Dogs allowed all year
D Disabled   Beach access via slipway

Directions: At Helston, follow the A3083 to the Lizard, approx 5 miles after Helston take the B3296 to Mullion, follow signs to cove.

Post Code: TR12 7ER
OS Grid Ref: SW667180

51 KYNANCE COVE

A beautiful typically Cornish cove, with a sandy beach running in and out of the rocky outcrops. Steep pathway and finally steps down to the beach.

Comments:
Strong currents and danger of being cut off at high tide.

Directions: At Helston take A3083, to the Lizard just after Lizard village turn right for Kynance Cove.

P Parking   One NT Car Park
T Toilets   Yes + Disabled
F Facilities Café
A Activities Swimming, Walking
S Safety   No Lifeguards
D Dogs   Banned Easter to Oct 1st
D Disabled   Access via road with permission from
             NT staff

Post Code: TR12 7PJ
OS Grid Ref: SW688132

---

52 KENNACK SANDS

A popular sandy beach with rocky outcrops and many rock pools to explore. Access via slipway.

Comments:
Huge surfing beach at low tide.

Directions: At Helston take A3083, and take left turn after air base. After Goonhilly turn first right to Kugger At Kugger turn left for Kennack Sands.

P Parking   Yes, by beach
T Toilets   Yes, but no Disabled
F Facilities Café/Shop
A Activities Swimming, Surfing
S Safety   Lifeguards in summer
D Dogs   West banned Easter to Oct 1st
             East allowed all year
D Disabled   Beach access

Post Code: TR12 7LT
OS Grid Ref: SW732164

53 MAENPORTH

This lovely sheltered sandy beach becomes very busy in the season, but has ample parking. Family run café and shop. Level access. Slipway.

Comments:
Wildlife Nature Reserve, Kayak School, Mountain Bike Hire, Massage, Archery.

P Parking	Yes + 500 space overflow
T Toilets	Yes + Disabled
F Facilities	Shop, Café, Fish Restaurant
A Activities	Swimming, Watersports
S Safety	Volunteer Lifeguards in summer
D Dogs	Banned Easter to Oct 1st
D Disabled	Beach access easy

Directions: Follow the A39 to Falmouth, past a reservoir. Turn right at next roundabout, continue through Mawnan Smith and turn down left side of Red Lion pub follow road to beach.

Post Code: TR11 5HN
OS Grid Ref: SW789295

54 SWANPOOL BEACH

A popular sandy beach with rock pools at low tide. Watersports' centre and Children's play area and Beach huts.

Comments:
Everything provided for a full day at the beach. Nature Reserve.

P Parking	Yes 450 spaces
T Toilets	Yes + Disabled
F Facilities	Shop, Café, Surf and Watersports' hire
A Activities	Surfing, Mini Golf
S Safety	No Lifeguards
D Dogs	Banned Easter to Oct 1st
D Disabled	Beach access easy

Directions: Take A39 through Falmouth to crossroads. Turn right signed beaches. Take next second right and follow road to Swanpool.

Post Code: TR11 5BG
OS Grid Ref: SW800312

55 GYLLYNGVASE BEACH – FALMOUTH

A popular sandy beach on the edge of Falmouth. Nearby is Pendennis Castle and Queen Mary's Gardens which offer relaxation and beautiful views.

Comments:
A great place to watch the huge tankers waiting to enter Falmouth.

Directions: Take A39 through Falmouth to crossroads, turn right signed "Beaches". Take next second left and follow road to Gyllngvase.

P Parking	Yes, 160 spaces	
T Toilets	Yes + Disabled	
F Facilities	Cafés, Shop, Hire shop	
A Activities	Surfing, Swimming	
S Safety	Lifeguards in summer	
D Dogs	Banned Easter to Oct 1st	
D Disabled	Beach access easy	

Post Code: TR11 4PA
OS Grid Ref: SW809316

---

56 CASTLE BEACH – FALMOUTH

Various beaches along the seafront some rocky, some sandy.

Comments:
Opposite Falmouth Hotel.

Directions: Through Falmouth on A39 to crossroads, turn right signed "Beaches". Take 2nd left past Gyllyngvase to Cliff Rd.

P Parking	Cliff Rd parking 80 spaces	
T Toilets	Yes by beach	
F Facilities	Shop/Café	
A Activities	Surfing, Swimming	
S Safety	No Lifeguards	
D Dogs	Banned Easter to Oct 1st	
D Disabled	Beach access via slipway	

Post Code: TR11 4NZ
OS Grid Ref: SW817321

57 SUMMERS BEACH – ST MAWES

Various beaches on waterfront of the Fal estuary, some sandy, some rocky. Slipway.

Comments:
Various small sandy spots along waterfront.

P Parking	One large car park
T Toilets	Yes + Disabled
F Facilities	Shops, Cafés, Restaurants
A Activities	Boat trips, Fishing
S Safety	No Lifeguards
D Dogs	Banned Easter to Oct 1st
D Disabled	Beach access via slipway

Directions: Approaching from east or west on A390, about 4 miles east of Truro turn onto A3078 for St Mawes.

Post Code: TR2 5DA
OS Grid Ref: SW841327

58 PORTHCURNICK

A wide sandy beach with rock pools, The beach is privately owned but access is allowed via steps from car park. Slipway at Rosevine.

Comments:
The beach is reached via a field and steep steps.

P Parking	Car park at Porthscatho – 5mins
T Toilets	Summer only, no Disabled
F Facilities	Shop in summer
A Activities	Swimming, Rock pooling
S Safety	No Lifeguards. Lifebuoy
D Dogs	Dogs allowed all year
D Disabled	No beach access

Directions: Take A390, approx 4 miles east of Truro, take A3078 for St Mawes. When you reach Trewithian turn left.

Post Code: TR2 5DL
OS Grid Ref: SW847331

59 TOWAN BEACH — NR GERRANS

A large relatively unknown beach made up of sand and shingle and backed by sand dunes, rock pools at either end, ideal for families with a picnic.

Comments:
Nearest villages Gerrans and Porthscatho. Beach is through gate opp Farmhouse

P Parking   NT car park
T Toilets   Yes + Disabled
F Facilities None
A Activities Swimming
S Safety   No Lifeguards
D Dogs   Dogs allowed all year
D Disabled   Beach access

Directions: Take A390, 4 miles east of Truro take A3078 for St Mawes. At Trewithian turn right for Gerrans and Porthcatho. Go through Gerrans past Trellice Holiday Park just after creek turn right into car park at Porth Farm.

Post Code: TR2 5EX
OS Grid Ref: SW866330

---

60 PENDOWER BEACH

A huge sandy beach, a mile long, one end of which is Carne Beach. Access via a slipway.

Comments:
Rock pools here have been designated Site of Scientific Interest.

P Parking   NT car park
T Toilets   Yes + Disabled at Carne
F Facilities Nare Hotel at Carne
A Activities Swimming, Surfing
S Safety   No Lifeguards
D Dogs   Dogs allowed all year on leads
D Disabled   Beach access

Directions: Take A390 and approx 4 miles east of Truro take A3078 for St Mawes. past Tregony and Ruan Highlanes. After the turning for Veryan take next left for Pendower.

Post Code: TR2 5PE
OS Grid Ref: SW898383

61 CARNE BEACH

A long sandy beach approx I mile long, one end of which is Pendower. Access via a slipway.

Comments:
Be aware that there can be a large swell at both beaches.

P Parking — NT car park
T Toilets — Yes + Disabled
F Facilities — Nare Hotel open to non-residents
A Activities — Swimming, Surfing
S Safety — No Lifeguards
D Dogs — Dogs allowed all year on leads
D Disabled — Beach access

Directions: Take A390, 4 miles east of Truro take A3078 for St Mawes go past Tregony and Ruan Highlanes. Turn left for Veryan At Veryan turn right then left then right again, follow road to Carne

Post Code: TR2 5PF
OS Grid Ref: SW90413

62 EAST PORTHOLLAND

A large sandy beach, level access at West Portholland and a slipway at East Portholland.

Comments:
Risk of rocks falling from cliffs.

P Parking — Yes by beach
T Toilets — Yes, but no Disabled
F Facilities — Café/Shop
A Activities — Swimming, Canoeing
S Safety — No Lifeguards. Lifebuoy
D Dogs — Dogs allowed all year
D Disabled — Steep slipway

Directions: At St Austell take B3273 to Mevagissey. After Pentewan, turn right for Gorran Haven, turn right for Highlanes then right for Caerhayes through Rescassa Turn right for Caerhays Castle, drive past Porthluney Beach to East Portholland.

Post Code: PL26 6NA
OS Grid Ref: SW960413

63 PORTHLUNEY COVE – CAERHAYES

A sheltered sandy beach, close to Caerhayes Castle and Gardens. Easy access to beach, rock pools at low tide. Very popular family beach.

Comments:
Caerhayes Castle is Victorian but is said to be built on the site of a medieval manor house.

P	Parking	Two car parks by beach
T	Toilets	Yes, Disabled access
F	Facilities	Café/Shop
A	Activities	Swimming, Canoeing
S	Safety	No Lifeguards
D	Dogs	Dogs allowed all year
D	Disabled	Beach access

Directions: At St Austell take B3273 to Mevagissey After Pentewan turn right for Gorran Haven through Highlanes then right for Caerhayes through Rescassa,right again for beach.

Post Code: PL26 6LX
OS Grid Ref: SX960413

64 PORTHPEAN BEACH – ST AUSTELL

The sandy beach slopes gently to the sea making this a popular beach for families. Access is good and sailing and boat launching facilities are available.

Comments:
Be aware that this beach shelves very quickly.

P	Parking	One large private car park
T	Toilets	Yes, Disabled in St Austell
F	Facilities	Café, Deckchair hire
A	Activities	Windsurfing, Sailing, Canoeing
S	Safety	No Lifeguards
D	Dogs	Banned Easter to Oct 1st
D	Disabled	Beach access

Directions: Approaching St Austell on A390 turn right for Porthpean. Follow this road and beach is down 2nd left turn.

Post Code: PL26 6AX
OS Grid Ref: SX030500

65 CARLYON BAY

The long sandy beach is privately owned and access is via the seafront. When building work is completed, this will be one of the most attractive beaches in Cornwall.

Comments:

Be aware that at the time of going to print this is a building site but with safe and attractive access to beach.

Directions: Take the Par turning off the A390 just east of St Austell and follow signs for Carlyon Bay.

Post Code: PL25 3RG
OS Grid Ref: SX056522

P Parking   One above beach
T Toilets   Yes but no Disabled
F Facilities Café
A Activities Boat hire, Children's play area
S Safety   No Lifeguards
D Dogs   Allowed all year
D Disabled No beach access until building completed

66 GORRAN HAVEN

A quiet family beach, two miles south of Mevagissey, protected by a stone harbour.

Comments:

Take care on way down to beach, lane is very narrow.

Directions: A390 from St Austell take B3273 for Mevagissey, shortly after Pentewan, turn right for Gorran Haven, follow this road to the beach.

Post Code: PL26 6JP
OS Grid Ref: SX013415

P Parking   Large field car park
T Toilets   Yes, but no Disabled
F Facilities Shop/Café in village
A Activities Fishing, Boating trips
S Safety   No Lifeguards
D Dogs   Allowed all year
D Disabled Beach access

PAR – ST AUSTELL

A wide sandy beach backed by sand dunes. This popular beach has plenty of sand left at high tide. Easy access.

Comments:
This beach shelves very gently for about ½ mile.

P	Parking	One large one by beach
T	Toilets	Yes, but no Disabled
F	Facilities	Shop, Café, Pub, Picnic area
A	Activities	Windsurfing, Bowling
S	Safety	No Lifeguards
D	Dogs	Allowed all year
D	Disabled	Beach access

Directions: Approach St Blazey on A390 Take B3082 through Par just after 2nd railway bridge, turn right into car park at Par Caravan Park.

Post Code: PL24 2AR
OS Grid Ref: SX088534

---

68 POLKERRIS

A small attractive harbour beach. This curved sandy beach is very popular with families with young children. Slipway.

Comments:
This is the home of the Polkerris Sailing School.

P	Parking	Yes, 4 mins from beach
T	Toilets	Yes, but no Disabled
F	Facilities	Shop, Café, Pub, Surf hire
A	Activities	Surfing, Sailing
S	Safety	No Lifeguards
D	Dogs	Banned Easter to Oct 1st
D	Disabled	Beach access via slipway

Directions: From A390, take B3269 for Fowey. Just before Fowey turn right at roundabout onto B3082 Take next left, then right follow road to Polkerris.

Post Code: PL24 2TL
OS Grid Ref: SX094524

(69) READYMONEY COVE – FOWEY

A small sandy cove, just on the Fowey Estuary. There are rock pools at low tide. Swimming raft. Slipway. Boat launch at Bodinnick.

Comments:
Great estuary views, overlooked by St Catherine's Castle.

P Parking   Two, above the town
T Toilets   Yes + Disabled
F Facilities   Shops, Café, Restaurants in Fowey
A Activities   Walking, Fishing
S Safety   No Lifeguards. Lifebouy
D Dogs   Banned Easter to Oct 1st
D Disabled   Beach access, drop off point

Directions: From A390, turn left onto B3269, at roundabout go straight across onto B3082. Take left exit at next two roundabouts. Follow directions to car parks.

Post Code: PL23 1JD
OS Grid Ref: SX117512

(70) POLPERRO

A small sandy beach beyond the harbour, also a tidal pool below the cliffs.

Comments:
Horse Bus and Tram down into village. Model village and smugglers museum.

P Parking   One, on approach to village
T Toilets   Yes + Disabled at Fisna Bridge
F Facilities   Café, Gift Shops, Museum
A Activities   Boat trips
S Safety   No Lifeguards
D Dogs   Banned 24/7
D Disabled   Beach access

Directions: Take A38 from Plymouth, at Trerulefoot. Turn left onto the A374. After approx 1 mile take left turn onto A387 for Looe. At Looe cross bridge and continue to Polperro, Follow signs to beach.

Post Code: PL13 2RD
OS Grid Ref: SX210509

www.polperro.com

LOOE – EAST BEACH

This sandy seafront beach is very popular with families. It slopes very gently making it safer for novice swimmers and young children.

Comments:
Sand Chair Hire. 01503 263709

P	Parking	At Discovery Centre, West Looe
T	Toilets	Yes + Disabled
F	Facilities	Shops, Cafés, Restaurants
A	Activities	Boat trips
S	Safety	No Lifeguards
D	Dogs	Banned all year - but allowed all year on Hannafore Beach
D	Disabled	Beach access

Directions: Take A38 from Plymouth. At Trerulefoot turn left onto A374, after approx. 1 mile turn right onto A387. On reaching Widegates take B3253 for Looe.

Post Code: PL13 1BU
OS Grid Ref: SX256531

SEATON

A spacious grey-sand and shingle beach. At low tide it joins onto Downderry Beach. Access level.

Comments:
Beach car park gets full, come early.

P	Parking	Two + Beach parking
T	Toilets	Yes + Disabled at Downderry
F	Facilities	Shop, Café, Pub
A	Activities	Surfing, Windsurfing
S	Safety	No Lifeguards
D	Dogs	Dogs allowed all year
D	Disabled	Beach access

Directions: Take A38 from Plymouth, at Trerulefoot turn left onto A374. After approx. 1 mile turn right onto A387 for Looe. Follow road to Hessonford and turn left. Continue on this road to Seaton.

Post Code: PL11 3JN
OS Grid Ref: SX302543

73 DOWNDERRY BEACH

A wide and spacious sand and shingle beach, backed by cliffs. Access via path alongside toilets or a slipway. The beach is sometimes an unofficial nudist beach.

Comments:
Risk of being cut off at high tide

 P Parking   Yes.
T Toilets   Yes + Disabled
F Facilities Café, Coffee shop
A Activities Fishing, Sailing, Canoeing
S Safety   No Lifeguards
D Dogs   Allowed all year
D Disabled   Beach access via slipway

Directions: Take A38 from Plymouth. At Trerulefoot turn left onto A374. After approx 1 mile turn right onto A387 for Looe. At Hessenford turn left and follow road to Seaton Valley Follow coast road to Downderry.

Post Code: PL11 3JY
OS Grid Ref: SX314539

74 PORTWRINKLE BEACH

Two sand and shingle beaches popular with families. Access poor steep steps. East beach used by experienced surfers.

Comments:
Unstable cliffs, bathing unsafe when low to medium tide.

P Parking   Two on cliff top
T Toilets   Yes, but no Disabled
F Facilities Refreshments in village
A Activities Surfing
S Safety   No Lifeguards - bathing can
            be dangerous
D Dogs   Banned Easter to Oct 1st
D Disabled   No beach access

Directions: Take A374 west from Torpoint. Turn left at Antony on B3247. Turn right at T-junction after a mile and then left beside Finnygook Inn. Follow road to beach.

Post Code: PL11 3BU
OS Grid Ref: SX359539

75 WHITSAND BAY

Four miles of perfect sand make this one of Cornwall's best beaches. Access very steep. Strong currents.

Comments:
Western end closed during firing range operations at Tregantle Fort. Firing times indicated by red flags.

P Parking	At Whitsand, Sharrow,Tregonhawke
T Toilets	Yes at Tregonhawke
F Facilities	Café at Tregonhawke
A Activities	Surfing
S Safety	Lifeguards in summer
D Dogs	Allowed all year
D Disabled	No beach access

Directions: Take A38 from Plymouth. At Trerulefoot, turn left A374, 2 miles after Polbathic take B3247 to Crafthole. At Crafthole turn left and continue on B3247. Badly signed car park just before Freathy.

Post Code: PL10 1JS
OS Grid Ref: SX399518

76 KINGSAND AND CAWSAND

Sand and shingle beaches with rock pools at Kingsand and access via slopes and steps. Cawsand access via slipway.

Comments:
Last beaches in Cornwall.

P Parking	Yes at both beaches.
T Toilets	Yes + Disabled Kingsand
F Facilities	Cafés, Restaurants, Gift shops
A Activities	Sailing, Windsurfing, Diving
S Safety	No Lifeguards
D Dogs	Dogs allowed all year at Kingsand. Banned Easter to Oct 1st at Cawsand
D Disabled	Beach access

Directions: Take A38 from Plymouth. At Trerulefoot turn left onto A374 2 miles after Polbathic turn right B3247 to Crafthole. At Crafthole turn left B3247 to Millbrook. After Millbrook, turn right onto beach road.

Post Code: PL10 1PJ
OS Grid Ref: SX431502

SAFETY FLAGS

 his flag indicates a patrolled beach

 his flag indicates a surfboard and craft zone NOT a safe place to swim

 his flag indicates that the beach is closed. DO NOT enter the water

SAFETY CODE

- Find the red and yellow flags and swim between them
- Look at safety signs
- Ask a lifeguard for advice
- Get a friend to swim with you
- Stick your hand up in the air and shout for help, if you are in trouble in the water

SUN SAFETY

- Limit time in the sun. Sun is at its strongest between 10am and 4pm
- Wear a hat and use sunglasses with 99-100% UVA and UVB protection. Use at least SPF 15-20 sunscreen. Higher on children. Reapply every 2 hours or after going in water

MILD SUNBURN: Mild sunburn can be treated at home

- Stay out of the sun after burning
- Have a cool shower or bath (not cold)
- Apply aftersun lotion
- Take in extra fluids for 2 or 3 days
- Take a painkiller for any pain
- Keep all sunburned areas covered until they are healed

SEVERE SUNBURN: Severe sunburn requires medical help. See a doctor if:

- Sunburn becomes blisters or is extremely painful
- If your face swells
- If you become feverish or have chills
- If you have severe head aches, faintness or confusion
- If you are dehydrated (feeling unusually thirsty)

MINOR INJURIES UNITS

BODMIN HOSPITAL 01208 251577
CAMBORNE AND REDRUTH HOSPITAL.........01209 881650
FALMOUTH HOSPITAL 01326 434700
FOWEY HOSPITAL...01726 832241
HELSTON HOSPITAL......................................01326 435815
LAUNCESTON HOSPITAL...............................01566 765653
LISKEARD HOSPITAL 01579 335278
NEWQUAY HOSPITAL....................................01637 893623
ST AUSTELL HOSPITAL.................................01726 291199
ST BARNABAS HOSPITAL SALTASH 01752 857407
ST MARY'S HOSPITAL SCILLY ISLES..............01720 422392
STRATTON HOSPITAL BUDE.........................01288 287713

If you are not sure if your injury requires a Minor Injury Unit or an A&E admission ring **NHS DIRECT 0845 4647**. The nurses there will decide which place you need to go to. If you go to **A&E** with a minor injury you will go to the back of the queue behind more serious cases. In a Minor Injury Unit you will usually be seen in the order you arrive. For broken bones check with the Minor Injury Unit if they have X-Ray equipment, if not go to **A&E**.

Not all MINOR INJURY UNITS are open 24/7 and you will need to dial 111 to check

A & E DEPARTMENTS:
Royal Cornwall Hospital, Treliske, Truro
Plymouth (Derriford) Hospital

Other useful numbers:
NHS Emergency Dental Treatment 01872 35437
Police (Emergency) 999
Police (Emergency from a mobile)............112 (this searches all networks for a signal)
Police Enquiries (Non-Emergency)..............08452 777444

BEACH TIPS

- Use beaches with Lifeguards, listen to their advice.
- Don't swim if the sea is rough; there are strong currents or rip currents.
- Don't swim for at least one hour after eating or drinking alcohol.
- Don't use inflatables in the sea, you could be swept out.
- Raise your arm to attract attention if you are in trouble. Shout for help, stay calm. Do exactly as your rescuer says. Relax and do not struggle.
- If you are caught in a rip current, Don't panic, swim parallel to the shore. Raise your arm to signal for help. Stay calm.
- Remember: Lifeguards are not kids with holiday jobs, they are trained professionals with a sound knowledge of the tides on the beaches they patrol. Listen to them; it could save your life.

BITES AND STINGS

Snake bites: They should always receive medical attention, don't waste time, get to hospital quickly. A description of the snake will help the staff at A&E.

Weaver Fish: They have an extremely painful sting, but do not usually need medical attention. Treatment: Alternate very cold and very hot water, soak sting area.

Jelly Fish: Large sting - seek medical advice.
Small sting - wrap cloth soaked in white vinegar around sting area. Painkillers may help.

CLIFF FALLS

Following the very wet summer of 2012 and the winter of 2012/13 there are warnings of cliff falls. Please take care both on the cliff paths and on beaches; take notice of warning signs and fencing.

MARINE RESCUE

Live Dolphins, Porpoises and Whales .... Tel. 01825 765 546

Live Seals — Seal Sanctuary .... Tel. 01326 221361
If dead — Cornwall Wildlife Trust .... Tel. 0845 201 2626

Lost and Found Dogs — RSPCA .... Tel. 01637 881455

SEALS — Pup (White and fluffy)

* Do keep your distance
* Don't handle it or stress it
* Don't put it back in the water
* Do ring the Seal Sanctuary
* Do only as they instruct
* Do try to assess its size accurately

It is rare to find a live fully grown seal, if you do ring the Seal Sanctuary.
If it's dead phone the Cornwall Wildlife Trust. Same rules apply.

WHALES, DOLPHINS AND PORPOISES

Same rules apply. Stay away even sick they can do a lot of harm.
Sick animals can be infectious, keep your distance and do not touch them.

ROYAL NATIONAL LIFEBOAT INSTITUTION (R.N.L.I.)

The RNLI is the charity that provides a 24 hour lifesaving service

TRAINING HEROES COSTS MONEY!

RNLI running costs are £402,000 per day.
For every £1 donated 85p goes to operations and 15p on generating income. It costs £1,266 per year to train a volunteer. Yes volunteer!!

The RNLI gets NO funding from the Government. It is funded entirely by your donations and the tireless work of fundraising volunteers all over the country.

If you would like to know how you can help, contact:
RNLI Greater London, 20 Buckingham Street, London WC2N 6EF
Tel: 020 7839 3369
E-mail: london@rnli.org.uk
Official Website: rnli.org.uk